T0329432

SCHOLARSHIP

ITS MEANING AND VALUE

SCHOLARSHIP
ITS MEANING AND VALUE

BY

H. W. GARROD

The J. H. Gray Lectures for 1946

CAMBRIDGE
AT THE UNIVERSITY PRESS
1946

CAMBRIDGE
UNIVERSITY PRESS

University Printing House, Cambridge CB2 8BS, United Kingdom

Published in the United States of America by Cambridge University Press, New York

Cambridge University Press is part of the University of Cambridge.

It furthers the University's mission by disseminating knowledge in the pursuit of
education, learning and research at the highest international levels of excellence.

www.cambridge.org
Information on this title: www.cambridge.org/9781107418691

© Cambridge University Press 1946

First published 1946
First paperback edition 2014

A catalogue record for this publication is available from the British Library

ISBN 978-1-107-41869-1 Paperback

I

IN *The Vanity of Human Wishes* Johnson gives a first place to the vanity of scholarship. Before the 'young enthusiast' commits himself to the life of learning, to scholarship as a profession, let him stop and think. Let him 'pause awhile from letters to be wise'—or, at any rate, worldly-wise. Let him mark the ills which assail the scholar's life. Johnson lists the more impressive of them:

Toil, envy, want, the patron, and the jail.

He might, I suppose, have added something about the scholar in the scullery. But he is interested in a more appealing figure, the scholar on the scaffold. Among the obvious prizes of scholarship is church-preferment. Not all scholars are as unlucky as Lydiat—though why Johnson puts Lydiat with the great scholars, I do not know, Lydiat of whom Scaliger[1] said that the world had never

[1] Epistolae 1627, ccxli. Lydiat's *De variis annorum formis* reached Scaliger at the time of the Leiden Fair in 1605. The great attraction of the Fair in that year was a troupe of English comedians; the whole town, including crowds of foreigners, rushed to see them. Scaliger stayed at home, reading Lydiat, whom he found more comic than any comedy (*Prolegomena in Canones*, 1658, iij^vo). I commend the passage

bred so big a fool. Lydiat had to put up with an Oxfordshire rectory. Yet not even 'the glittering eminence' of a bishopric can be thought exempt from peril. Johnson admonishes his scholar to remember how 'fatal learning' led Laud to the block. Macaulay's comment is unforgettable, and perhaps unforgivable: 'Laud, a poor creature who never did, said, or wrote anything indicating more than the ordinary capacity of an old woman.' But what is the matter, in truth, with Johnson's scholar is that he is insufficiently disinterested. He seeks truth, certainly—he is interested rather specially in religious truth. So far he has (we might know he would have) Johnson's best prayers:

And Virtue guard thee to the Throne of Truth.

But the Throne of Truth is not too sharply distinguished from the episcopal throne. Of learning as an end in itself, of a scholarship which is its own reward, Johnson has nothing to say. The world which he knew was a world where men worked for money, and wrote for money; if they alleged other motives they lied.

The first sketch for his picture of the scholar

to the attention of the students of Elizabethan Drama—I do not find it noted in the chapter on 'English Players on the Continent' in Chambers' *Elizabethan Stage*.

was made in the year in which Bentley died. If not when he made the first sketch, yet certainly when he made the finished picture, Johnson had Bentley in mind. Yet oddly enough, not Bentley the scholar; but a Bentley hard to believe in, Bentley the poet. A one-poem poet, it is true; but the same person as the scholar. There is nobody in the world, says Chesterton somewhere, who has not at some time or other written poetry —unless, he adds weakly, it be Mr Bernard Shaw. Shaw in truth wrote a whole play in blank verse, for a reason which he gives himself—he found it much easier than prose. Bentley wrote one poem, and one only. But it was a good poem, and a fortunate one: it had the happy fortune to be read and admired by Johnson. Without it, we should not have had the lines on the scholar in *The Vanity of Human Wishes.* Why our Johnsonians have missed Johnson's source, I cannot guess; for the likeness of the two sets of verses is notable. Bentley's verses are not so well known but that I may be forgiven for quoting them entire.

i

Who strives to mount Parnassus *Hill,*
And thence Poetick Laurels bring,
Must first acquire due Force and Skill,
Must fly with Swan's, or Eagle's, Wing.

ii

Who Nature's Treasures would explore,
  Her Mysteries and Arcana know,
Must high, as lofty Newton, *soar,*
  Must stoop, as searching Woodward, low.

iii

Who studies ancient Laws and Rites,
  Tongues, Arts and Arms, all History,
Must drudge like Selden, *Days and Nights,*
  And in the endless Labour dye.

iv

Who travels in Religious Jars,
  (Truth mixt with Errors, Shade with Rays,)
Like Whiston, *wanting* Pyx *and Stars,*
  In Ocean wide or sinks, or strays.

v

But grant our Heroe's Hopes, long Toil,
  And comprehensive Genius, crown,
All Sciences, all Arts, his Spoil,
  Yet what Reward, or what Renown?

vi

Envy innate in vulgar Souls,
  Envy steps in, and stops his Rise;
Envy with poison'd Tarnish fouls
  His Lustre, and his Worth decrys.

Inglorious, or by Wants inthrall'd,
  To Colledge, and old Books, confin'd,
A Pedant from his Learning call'd,
  Dunces advanc'd, he's left behind;
Yet left Content, *a Genuine* Stoick *He,*
  Great *without* Patron, rich *without* South-Sea![1]

Johnson, we know from Boswell, had Bentley's
poem by heart. For Bentley, it was a Horatian
exercise; written to admonish a 'youthful enthusiast',[2] to whom scholarship seemed (what
Bentley knew it not to be) roses all the way. Toil,
envy, want, the patron, and—if not the jail—the
austerities of Trinity College: all these Bentley
knew. But he knew also, what Johnson hardly
suspects, an ultimate contentment that there is in
scholarship. A stoical contentment, admittedly.
But in his concluding couplet Bentley does honour,
what Johnson omits, the genuineness of the life of
scholarship, its greatness not dependent upon
patronage, its satisfactions of internal wealth. That
scholarship is, like virtue, its own reward, that
what the world does for the scholar, does not

[1] *The Grove,* 1721, pp. 247–9. There are slightly different
versions in *The Gentleman's Magazine,* 1740, p. 616, and
Dodsley's Collection 1758, VI, 160–1. In V, 1–2 I have
adopted Dodsley's punctuation.

[2] Dodsley gives his name—'Mr Titley'. See Monk's
Life of Bentley, p. 470.

matter, he is too honest to say—too honest, for he has been too often disappointed.

What the world does for the scholar *does* perhaps matter. That it should consign good scholars to the scullery, and bad ones to the deanery, is bad. Yet what the scholar does for the world, what his just place is in the army of human helpers, this too matters, and is not so obvious but that the world may be forgiven if it sometimes makes mistakes. We must allow to the world, in any case, its proper prejudices. Among these may be reckoned a prejudice for the *genialities*. Learning, consummate learning, is a thing a good deal more rare than genius. But in comparison with genius—such is the world, such is life—the odds are always, and everywhere, against it. For one thing, it is a good deal less intelligible than genius. And this, partly, from the very rarity with which its perfections manifest themselves. In a university, if anywhere, one might expect to know it familiarly. I have lived in one for fifty years. I should not be believed anywhere but in Oxford —and perhaps Cambridge—if I said, what is, even so, true, that I have known genius familiarly; talking with it—or at least being talked to by it— endlessly, understanding it easily, sometimes even seeing through it; but consummate learning I have met only very rarely, conversing with it uncomfortably, and often not well knowing what it would be at. Nor is it merely that learning manifests itself less often than genius. It has the further disadvantage that, when it does manifest itself, it can be known only by its like. Mediocrity can appreciate genius. Everywhere its effects are at once apprehended. It is sensibly known in the quickening of the blood, the tension of the nerves, the fine thrill of the whole being. It accomplishes its end in being felt. There is a sense in which genius, mysterious as it is, is the most intelligible of all things. Learning is at once less direct in its aims, and more obscure in its effects. There is nothing in the method of it by which it can capture the heart of the world. Men admire what is great most of all when it seems to be done easily; and the mark of genius is its divine facility. It may endure agonies, but it does not take pains. Learning must both take pains and give them.

The unhappiness of learning Johnson, I must think, exaggerates; Bentley here is better informed. The unhappiness of genius we somehow take for granted. At least I like to think it is never so unhappy as it looks. Yet genius and learning have, I must think, a common trouble; a common trouble arising from a not very obvious community of ideal. The end which genius and learning alike seek and miss, moving by different paths to their common disappointment, may be said, perhaps, in language not too grandiloquent, to be the restoration of a broken unity of the human spirit. To genius, this broken unity appears mainly as a moral and personal disaster. To learning it presents itself as an intellectual trouble. There are gaps and fissures in the culture of nations; accidents of time, language, place and race hinder sympathy and understanding; after all effort, there remains a pitiful discontinuity in the movement of the human mind. We hear the cry of the past; but we reach out hands in vain to our spiritual kindred. They cannot come to us, nor our weak faculties fly to them. It is because genius and learning conceive thus differently the trouble which affects them, because the one views it as an accident of time, the other as a property of the soul—it is because of this that there commonly appears in either a certain impatience of the method of the other. The two stand contrasted somewhat as the method of storm and the method of siege; and the world sides naturally with the battle of the swift, with the spiritual valour which dashes itself to pieces on the unbreachable walls which fence Truth. The slow and cautious movement of learning has little in it to fascinate eye or heart, and will rarely command from the crowd more than that cool approval which salutes mediocrity. The two activities are conceived as antithetical. We pit Imagination against Knowledge, Letters against Science, the Poet against the

Scholar; and in the very act of doing so we are fighting against the cause for which these contrasted causes exist—the unity of the human spirit.

It was not always so, perhaps; at any rate, the antithesis was not always quite so keenly felt. There was a period in the world's history, and a period of some extension, when the repute of learning was hardly inferior to that of genius, a period in which the two activities were not conceived as mutually exclusive. It is easier to say when it ended than when it began. It might plausibly be contended that it began with the beginning of letters. But if anybody prefers to date its beginnings from the rebirth of letters, from the Renaissance, I am not here much concerned. I am more concerned to date the close of it. The close of it is marked, I think, by the early years of the seventeenth century. The last great name in it I take to be that of the younger Scaliger. At his death in 1609 Josephus Justus Scaliger was the greatest scholar in Europe. But he was a good deal more. He was a force in European letters and life. Princes and parliaments paid court to him. The Church feared him. To the learned he was a god—*vir divinus* Casaubon calls him. Young men recorded in their note-books, for the benefit of after ages, his casual utterances. In what concerned literary reputation his every word was a fate—*vocem fata sequuntur*. No scholar, as such, will ever hold again a like primacy. The conditions of it have passed beyond hope of recall. Of the manner of their passing I will speak more fully later. I will note here one or two circumstances in connexion with it which are of particular significance.

When Scaliger was born, modern literature was, outside Italy, almost non-existent. When he died, the world was already the richer by nearly all the greatest works of Shakespeare. His fame was contemporary with that of Ronsard and the Pleiad. French verse was just beginning to contend with Latin. Du Bellay had used Latin to achieve a wider hearing. Dorat, the teacher of Ronsard, and himself one of the Pleiad, was a poet—a voluminous one—only in Greek and Latin. A matter of months, again, separates the death of Scaliger from the birth of Milton. Milton's reputation crossed the continent only as that of a Latin pamphleteer. It was a chance that *Paradise Lost* was not written in Latin. *Paradise Lost* was edited later by the scholar who may fairly be regarded as the most considerable that Europe has produced since Scaliger—Bentley. As a boy Bentley might have talked with Milton. What had passed in Europe between Scaliger and Bentley is strangely brought home to us when we find Bentley emending the text of *Paradise Lost* as Scaliger had emended that of Catullus, Propertius, Tibullus, and Manilius. It is instructive also to observe that that work of Bentley by which he is still, and quite justly, most famous—a masterpiece with many of the great qualities of Scaliger's masterpiece, the *Emendatio Temporum*—it is instructive to observe that the *Letters of Phalaris* is written in English. It is the first great work of scholarship to appear in a vernacular tongue. To the controversy out of which it arose we owe Swift's *Battle of the Books*, a satire of which the historical importance is at least equal to the literary merit. The issues which it debates affect the prestige, not only of the scholar, but of the authors themselves whom he seeks to interpret. It requires some effort of mind, when we read it, to persuade ourselves that, a bare century earlier, Scaliger was talking with kings, while the most transcendent genius of modern Europe held horses' heads at the door of a suburban theatre.

In a sense, wherever we have letters, there we have scholarship. We might intelligibly call Homer a scholar—we have heard often enough that he is a school. Homer holds to a tradition—he has that consciousness of relation to a previous art which is a principal character of Scholarship. But so has every artist save the first, every man of letters that has not fallen from the moon. What matters is the degree and the manner in which this consciousness operates. In degree, it must operate, if we are to use the term Scholarship appropriately, to the extent of overshadowing the free sense of creative power. In manner it must so operate as to reveal a felt discontinuity in the line of development between study and its object. Only so is there Scholarship, except in distant similitude. There may be periods of observation and analysis, which have many of the character-istics of Scholarship. There may be grammatical, or literary, or antiquarian study. But there will not be Scholarship in the sense in which we use the word of the studies of the Renaissance, or of modern scholarship.

Homer is not a scholar, nor yet Plato, nor even Aristotle. Aristotle has no consciousness of any broad dividing line which estranges him from the great writers whose art he criticizes so coldly. No sword has pierced the unity of intellectual develop-ment which he envisages. The contrast here with the Alexandrians, with whom, if there are any beginnings, scholarship begins, is real. The line which separates the 'scholarship' of Aristotle from that of Aristarchus is at once broader and deeper than that which divides Aristarchus and Bentley. The Alexandrians are the first Greeks to feel a division between themselves and that mighty order of things which gave birth to the masterpieces of Hellenic art and literature. Between Aristotle and Aristarchus the whole perspective of criticism has changed. The disruption of the old Greek City-State, and, with it, of the conditions out of which Greek literature arose, has put a false distance—which is yet a very real one—between the Alexandrians and the objects of their study. Habituation to a foreign court has made the life which Greek literature mirrors recede to a point where perfect sympathy can be retained, or recaptured, if at all, only by close attention and by an effort of the historical imagination. It is important here to remember that the Greeks were, in one respect, singularly deficient in literary experience. They had never habituated themselves to the study of any literature save that which reflected their own temperament—whatever did not do that was 'barbarian'. It was not easy, therefore, for the Alexandrian scholars to hold, by the historical imagination, a fugitive Hellenism, a life and art which seemed to be slipping away insensibly. For that was their task.

Of many benefits which Alexandrian scholarship conferred upon the world, it must suffice here to recall one only. Alexandria gave the world its first lesson in the practical organization of knowledge. To collect together into one place all the books worth having, to transcribe purified texts, to make these, by cataloguing and indexing, easily accessible—to-day all this seems a simple and obvious behaviour. That it was the most obvious use of princely wealth it required, perhaps, in the third century B.C., princely imagination to discover. Nor did the Ptolemies design the Libraries of Alexandria to be repositories of an inert learning. They wished that they should be, and they had the wealth and imagination to make them, a focus of intellectual life, a centre of that co-operative reflexion without which talent is desultory and genius provincial. Creating the first great Library, they created at the same time the first university. All the familiar types of don are there; a third-century satirist[1] compares the Museum of Alexandria to a hencoop, full of perpetually squabbling bibliomaniacs and scribblers, feeding, feeding, and half of them foreigners. Genius and learning, however, it is worth noticing, were not yet conceived in utter antithesis. The scholar and the poet, often enough, were a single character. To the Alexandrians, then, we owe both our libraries and our universities, and the first example of that function of scholarship which is its most important activity—the effort, in an

[1] Timon of Phlius; see Athenaeus, 22 D.

age of transition or disruption, to hold together the frayed threads of the spiritual life, to relate a new order to one dying or dead. This Alexandria did in that age of Greek depression which followed the collapse of the City-State. In a less degree, and in a fashion different and more indirect, it did it again in the period of transition from the pagan to the Christian world. Of its influence in this period we can form only an uncertain picture. But it was to the East, and to Alexandria among other cities of the East—Antioch, Edessa, Nisîbis —that the monasteries of the West—of Gaul and of the Italian islands—owed the institution of their *scriptoria*, the writing-rooms which later became universal in monastic foundations and in which were copied those remains of ancient literature which have survived to us from the storms of the Middle Ages.

We call the Alexandrians scholars, and their claim to be so called is logical and intelligible. To the Romans, again, who were in large part their pupils, we may intelligibly concede the same title. Indeed, so native to the Roman temper was the spirit of antiquarianism that we are tempted sometimes to think of the great writers of Rome as of a race of scholars, men versed in the prudence of literature but never attaining its joy and genius. The kind of learning, however, which is familiarly and naturally called in this country scholarship (and in other countries philology) may fairly be regarded as the invention of the Renaissance. We may, if we like—and logically, no doubt, we should—go behind the Renaissance. Yet the men of the Renaissance are more truly scholars than any who preceded them in that they were more profoundly conscious of that broken unity of the human spirit the sense of which is a distinguishing character of scholarship. They sought to recover a lost life. It was the task of their scholarship, as it is of ours—and it is this which marks off both our learning and theirs from that of Greece and Rome—to recover from the scattered fragments of a literature and language long dead the form and spirit of antiquity.

We have no word in English—we have to borrow a French word, to designate that great period of stir and awakening, of the rising up and flourishing of the long-dormant energies of western Europe, which we call the Renaissance. It may be that we are not, as the French are, with their genius for mutation, forever expectant of a new birth of the world. We are so much accustomed, it may be, to human nature at its normal level, and so little displeased with it, that, outside material achievement, we rarely—save perhaps in religion—credit it with the daring, the enthusiasm, the magnificence which it from time to time astonishes us by manifesting in history. Its possibilities of superb life touch us only distantly. But this word, which the French have lent to us, expresses truly the meaning, to those who inaugurated it, of the great movement which it designates. The Renaissance was nothing less than a new birth. It is bare truth to say that the movement out of which sprang what we call scholarship sought, not learning, but life. The beginnings of this movement go back to the middle of the fourteenth century: it was in 1333 that Petrarch made at Liège the first of his famous Ciceronian discoveries. But Scholarship, as we still practise it, may conveniently be dated from the first decades of the fifteenth century. The scholar of this period whose character and achievements are best known to us is perhaps Poggio. He had not so deep a sense as some of his contemporaries of the inner meaning of the great movement of which he was so eminent an instrument. Yet he is greater than any of them in the genius (for there is such a thing) of discovery. Nor has any one of them quite the same freshness of mind, the same childlike enthusiasm, or an equal share of that indefinable quality of *gusto* which covers nearly all literary sins. In none of them, again, are the faults of the movement more clearly present to us. He is interesting to Englishmen for the two years which he spent in England in the service of Cardinal Beaufort. In his letters from England he has little good to say about it. Thrice he laments that he cannot manage to get to Oxford.

Poggio was born in 1380, six years after the death of Petrarch, and he died in 1459, five years after the birth of the greatest of the later humanists, Politian, and six years before the date of the earliest printed edition[1] of a classical author. These dates are not without significance. Poggio inherits from Petrarch his passion for the discovery of MSS., and the temper which regards such discovery as a discovery not merely of literature but of life. To Politian he hands on the tradition, which he founded, of the careful collation and ingenious emendation of texts. He was famous also for an art which the scholar to-day is content, and can perhaps afford, to neglect, but which in that age was highly esteemed—calligraphy. He copied MSS. himself with fine care. He took infinite pains in forming the handwriting of diligently selected scribes, multiplying correct and legible copies of his authors. Many specimens of his own handwriting survive, and it is one of the clearest and most elegant of the time. He and his

[1] Cicero, *De Officiis* and *Paradoxa*, printed by Fust and Schoeffer at Maintz in 1465.

friends and their copyists wrote what was called 'lettera antica'. They organized, that is, in an age of illegible handwritings, a return to the hands of the tenth and eleventh centuries—to a pattern of writing devised in the schools of Charlemagne, the so-called Caroline minuscule. And here they helped the world, and their fame, more than they knew. Living for 'good letters', dying just before the birth of printing, they lived on in their beautiful handwritings, which furnished the models for the earliest types set.

Poggio is the founder of modern scholarship in that he is the first editor—or rather, like Aldus Manutius i and Henry Stephanus, he is editor, printer, and publisher in one. He bequeathed to his successors three valuable legacies: the belief in ancient literature as a quickening force, the tradition of a fine critical discernment, and the practice of the *imitatio veterum*. In the imitation of the ancient models he was surpassed by those who came after him. Yet his Latin, though, judged by more modern standards, not always correct or appropriate, is extraordinarily lively and readable, and by his contemporaries was admired for its classicism.

The Renaissance was a revolt of the imaginative reason. Of literature of the imagination there was in Europe, outside the ancient writers, almost none. Dante, Petrarch, Boccaccio exhaust the great names. The human imagination crying to be fed could find sustenance only in the remains of Greece and Rome. These remains were for the most part rare and inaccessible; and on this account the first task of the scholar was discovery. We to-day can hardly recreate to our minds the joy of discovery as it exalted the first generation of scholars. Some faint image of it may descend upon us from the Letters of Poggio, or of Petrarch himself. Or in times nearer to our own, a distant analogue may be fetched, perhaps, from some fortunate experience of the archaeologist, the papyrologist, a Schliemann, an Evans, a Grenfell. Yet I am not sure but that Keats' sonnet upon Homer furnishes the true and full similitude. What some new planet is to the watcher of the sky, what the first sight of some untravelled sea is to the adventurous seaman—all that, and more, to these first scholars was each new author whom they brought from darkness into light. Small wonder that they gave so much of their time to correcting and improving these precious texts, or that they attached so high a value to the successful imitation of them. In considering their sedulous practice of composition, it must be remembered, of course, that Latin was the only common speech of educated men: that in Italy the Tuscan dialect, soon to prevail everywhere, had as yet a limited diffusion: that these Italians were seeking to recover the speech of their fathers. These reflexions, it is true, while they help us to understand the origins of scholarship, hardly render more intelligible the condition in which we find it to-day.

But let us see Poggio for a moment in a situation in which he is less at home than among his copying-clerks, a situation pregnant, as will appear, with issues momentous for scholarship. In 1403 he had entered the service of the Papal Chancery—a service in which he was engaged for exactly half a century, obedient to no less than seven Popes—masters of very different opinions, character, and fortune. In that service he was present at the most extraordinary assembly which ever came together to debate great European issues—the Council of Constance. It was in Constance that he encountered Cardinal Beaufort. The issues debated by the Council were really great —and yet to-day they seem almost Gilbertian. The mighty men of Christendom sat down in Constance to determine (*inter alia*) how they should deal with the unusual phenomenon of three simultaneously infallible Popes, each of whom out of his own infallibility was disposed to regard his rival as Antichrist. Incidentally this great international congress burnt at the stake first John Huss and then his friend Jerome of Prague. Poggio was present at, and has left a vivid description of, the trial and execution of Jerome.[1] In his narrative we behold the first contact of the Renaissance with the Reformation. Poggio makes no attempt to conceal his admiration for the eloquence, the infinite skill in debate, the lofty bearing of Jerome. 'He uttered no word not worthy of a good man. Indeed, if he felt truly what he spoke so eloquently there could be found in him not only no just cause for death but no ground even for the least offence.' 'There he stood, unfearing, unflinching, contemning, and even inviting, death. You would have thought him another Cato. Truly a man worthy of the immortal memory of the world!' And then he adds hastily: 'If his opinions were really hostile to the institutions of the Church, of course I do not praise that. But his learning I must admire, his eloquence, his suave pleading, his skill in reply.' The appeal of Jerome, in truth, is that he makes the Greek and Roman world credible. 'I confess', says Poggio, 'that I never saw a man on trial for his life who came so near to the grand accents of antiquity, the antiquity you and I so much admire.' And when Jerome faces the last issue, and

[1] *Poggii Epistolae*, I, ii, Florence, 1832.

the only eloquence left is to die well, what moves Poggio is, not holy dying, the beauty of martyrdom, but death keeping ancient quality. 'With gay front and cheerful countenance he moved to the last act. No fear had he of fire, of any torture, nor of death. Never was any Stoic of so great constancy, so gallant to meet desired death.'

The moral which Poggio draws from a scene by which (despite some wish to use it for the display of his own literary gift) he is genuinely moved, is characteristic. It is idle for persons like himself—for mere scholars—to endeavour to determine right and wrong in these high and perplexed matters. 'It is not for me', he writes, 'to judge so great a cause. I acquiesce in the judgements of men who are thought wiser than I am—Acquiesco eorum sententiis qui sapientiores habentur.' *Acquiesco!* And so he leaves Jerome of Prague, and carries his thoughts to Pope John XXIII, wondering idly whether Jerome is 'vir bonus', and perfectly well aware that John XXIII is such a prodigy of vice and impiety as would be incredible if it were not a part of the history of the Papacy. This letter is the noblest and most eloquent that Poggio ever wrote. Yet in it there stands clearly revealed the weakness of the whole movement of Italian scholarship—its defect of intellectual power.

II

PERHAPS only one Italian escapes this condemnation—Poggio's enemy Laurentius Valla. I call him Poggio's enemy. But the grounds of hostility between them were inconceivably trivial. A pupil of Valla's had scrawled in the margin of a copy of Poggio's Letters some unfavourable comments upon their Latinity. Poggio supposed the offending comments to be those, not of the pupil, but of the master. There ensued a war of pamphlets scurrilous and obscene beyond belief. Beyond belief is it, and yet it happened, that Valla's obscenities, *libri quatuor*, were dedicated to Pope Nicholas V. The affair would not be worth attention, were it not that we sometimes forget the origins of scurrility in scholarship. When we are shocked by the savageries of Scaliger; when we are shocked—and more deeply—by those interchanged between Salmasius and Milton; when we are shocked (if we are) by the asperities of Bentley or Housman, we may usefully recall, perhaps, that this inhumanity of humanism harks back to the beginnings of scholarship. Nor are scholars the only offenders in this kind. Religion is often as beastly as scholarship. So is politics; and with less excuse, for in politics there are no heresies, nor do we look for good grammar.

Valla, though he died two years before Poggio, was his junior by a whole generation. But in the character of his scholarship he belongs rather to the sixteenth than to the fifteenth century. He is the forerunner of Erasmus, and in some respects he anticipates Scaliger. Astonishing as was the variety of his accomplishment, still more astonishing was his independence of mind and critical insight. He began his literary career with an essay upon Pleasure and the True Good, cast in the form of a dialogue, and remarkable not only for the realistic quality which informs its style, but also for its bold challenge to received opinions. Christianity is pitted against Stoicism and Epicureanism, getting what must be called at best a narrow win. Valla followed this with a work upon Logic, usually known as the *Quaestiones Dialecticae*, of a character equally challenging. Here sounds the first trumpet in the war of humanism against the schoolmen. A later work, *Upon the Freedom of the Will*, rounds off a philosophic achievement which was one day to influence no less a man than Leibnitz. Between the dialogue upon Freewill and the Dialectical Questions Valla interposed a work of pure scholarship, to which he gave the somewhat misleading title *Elegantiae*. The ideal of this work is the discovery, not of fine style, but of good style; of a style, that is to say, which shall be truthful. The barbarisms propagated into Latin by the Middle Ages are bad, not so much because they are barbarisms as because they obscure or falsify what they set out to express. Bad Latin is so because it involves us in bad philosophy, bad theology, bad law—the lawyers hated Valla quite as much as the theologians did. The scholarship of the *Elegantiae*—and Valla's scholarship generally —is practical. Elegance for Valla consists in the normal clear Latin of the best writers, with careful avoidance, not only of barbarism, but of what is rare, strained, or bizarre. The same practicality, the same demand for clearness and truthfulness distinguishes Valla as a textual critic. As a textual critic, he is best seen, perhaps, in his notes upon Livy. More interesting to us, and, indirectly, of the first importance, is his work upon the Vulgate of the New Testament; if only for the influence which it exercised upon Erasmus. It is not in any sense a fundamental work; in some respects it is not even ambitious. It is limited by the practical aim of making the New Testament more intelligible. Yet here, as elsewhere, it is precisely Valla's strong instinct for the intelligible that makes him great—this, and the independence of mind which is the corollary to it. In the folio edition of his works printed at Basle in 1640, his Notes upon the New Testament are prefaced by Erasmus' letter to Chr. Fisher. The letter belongs to the year 1505; Fisher was an Englishman at the Papal Court, where he held the office of Protonotary. Within fifteen months of writing it, Erasmus left England for Italy, depositing with Colet a new Latin version which he had made of the whole of the New Testament. He had made it while fresh from the influence of Valla. It was copied fair by one of Colet's scribes, Peter Meghen. Peter Meghen had one eye only; but it directed five accomplished fingers. Of the three volumes of his beautiful manuscript the first may still be seen in the Cambridge University Library. 'With all who love good letters', Erasmus writes to Fisher, 'Valla's name should be, not as it once was, hated, but loved and venerated; for in his zeal for the restoration of letters he, well knowing what he was doing, played a part which exposed him to men's bitter hatred.'

Bolder, more immediately decisive, more obviously fundamental, was a quite different work of Valla, the so-called 'declamation' *De Falso Credita Et Ementita Constantini Donatione*. With this he achieved what is regarded to-day, I suppose, as his most splendid success. The work was an open attack upon the pretensions of the Papacy, and upon the whole fabric of the temporal power. Valla's supreme merit is, indeed, his gift of penetrating falsity and absurdity. It is his delight in the exercise of this gift, and not any reforming zeal, which everywhere determines his activity. The temporal power, the religious orders, the Vulgate, bad Latin generally, Aristotle, Aquinas, Cicero, the received systems of metaphysic and morals—Valla calls them all in question, and all in the same spirit—the spirit of scholarship, void of partisanship, void, it may be, of religious fervour, and even of reverence, but rejoicing in its own clarity and life. The pursuit of truth appeared to Valla merely as the most *natural* of occupations, and not as a crusade. He had no intention of dying for it; protected, indeed, by a powerful king, he could afford to be gay. Neither he nor the Pope nor, it is probable, his enemies took very seriously the accusations of heresy which were brought against him. It excited no surprise among his contemporaries that he ended his days in the pay of the Roman curia. A Roman cardinal—Bellarmine—called him 'the forerunner of Luther'. A more obvious affinity is with Erasmus.

In Italy Valla stands alone. He is the founder of an intellectual, as opposed to an aesthetic, or stylistic, scholarship. To the criticism of form he adds the criticism of matter; to the sense of beauty the instinct for knowledge. But in his own country, perhaps by his own fault, he has no disciples. The main line of Italian scholarship passes, without traversing Valla, to the scholar in whom, towards the end of the fifteenth century, it attains its most perfect character, Politian. What strikes us before anything else about the scholarship of Politian is its completeness. Prior to Politian Italian learning had been mainly a Latin learning. The founder of Greek study in Italy had been the Byzantine Chrysoloras, who had died during the Council of Constance. He had taught Poggio, Franciscus Barbarus, Marsuppinus, and others of the early humanists. A considerable impulse had been given to Greek scholarship, somewhat later, by the Congress of the Eastern and Western churches in 1438–9. One of the Greek scholars who attended that Congress was Gemistus Plethon; and to the enthusiasm inspired by his discourses Italy owed the foundation of the Platonic Academy of Florence. But a more important event was destined shortly to give a yet more decisive direction to Greek influence. This was the fall of Constantinople. It was at one time the fashion to ascribe to this event the whole impulse of the revival of Hellenism in Europe;

and the error has behind it the authority of Scaliger.[1] To-day, by a natural reaction we tend, perhaps, to underestimate the importance of this event; which was a great, if not an originative, force. Constantinople fell in 1453. The year following is that in which Politian was born. Politian studied Greek under Argyropoulos and Andronicus Callistus. He is the first European scholar to earn in full measure the praise of being *utriusque linguae doctus.* Indeed, he transcends that merit; for in the vernacular poetry of Italy he is held to be a not unworthy successor to Petrarch. He is called, upon his tombstone, 'the Angel with one head and three tongues'. The one head carried more learning than any Italian had previously possessed. He composed with facility in Greek, with feeling—and even with genius—in Latin. To the art of interpretation he brought delicacy and perception. One might wonder at first sight what the subsequent course of scholarship could add to this completeness.

Yet defects there are. To Poggio and his friends, scholarship was life—they rejoiced in it almost after the fashion of children. With Politian, classical studies are, rather, a garnish of life; his joy is a little tinged with academicism. To Valla, again, scholarship was truth, the truth about things

[1] See the dedication to the *Cyclometrica.*

that matter. In the age-long war of scholarship upon imposture and superstition he is one of our most gallant soldiers. Politian's scholarship wants intellectual quality; ultimate things do not concern him. His enemies reported him as saying that he had never read any book of the Scriptures twice. It was not true: though that he preferred the Odes of Pindar to the Psalms of David may have been true. Nor was it true, perhaps, that he was an infidel. Not for him either the grand infidelities or the grand fidelities! The temper which went to Valla's New Testament studies had no interest for him. If he had lived to see the New Testament of Erasmus, he would not have taken sides. He lived to see Savonarola dominant in Florence. But Savonarola was merely unintelligible to him. He had taught Reuchlin; a paradoxical contact with the Reformation. But in truth, this perfect scholar had no idea of the tremendous issues towards which scholarship was moving. His work is related consciously to none of the great needs of his own time, save the general refinement of life and manners. The very elegance of his learning has something of triviality; of that triviality which was presently to be the ruin of Italian scholarship. We detect in it the beginnings of a development which culminates in Muretus, and was not stayed till Scaliger.

The lives of Poggio and Valla fall outside, the life of Politian (which was short) falls just within, the era of printing. The early period of printed books was in some ways not wholly favourable to the advance of scholarship. It diffused knowledge, as knowledge had not been diffused before. But at the same time it to some extent arrested freedom. The splendid volumes of Aldus and Stephanus, while they pleased the eye, disarmed the critical conscience. The fair appearance of a finely typed page had in it something lulling. Some of the early printed books were the work of scholars. Many of them were not so, but were produced in haste, without any wide survey of the material available, with little regard for critical principles, and sometimes without much conscience. It must be remembered that an inferior text has, in print, a tenacity of badness which does not belong to a manuscript. Not only is a single bad book printed, the equal numerically of a thousand or more bad MSS., but, once it has been produced, it tends to act as a deterrent to rival ventures. Fixity of text, moreover, tends to stereotype opinion and ideas. The period, accordingly, which lies between Politian and Scaliger is, in many ways, a static period in scholarship. It is a period of desultory commentation, lazy conjecture, and idle and unending verse-making. The old conception of literature as the mistress of life has failed from out the ideal of scholarship. Nor is it yet haunted by any historic sense of the greatness and *wholeness* of antiquity. Mostly, it has two ends only in view; the one to minister to the vanity of its creators, the other to produce handbooks for the classroom. One or two men—in France, for example, Turnebus and Lambinus—set their faces towards a higher ideal. But even they do not escape the infection of a period in which the typical name is that of the French-Italian Muretus.

Nevertheless, the period is one in which mighty forces are working mightily; and the beginning of it is distinguished by a name of which the splendour is, after four centuries, hardly at all diminished in Europe. We have beheld Poggio in Constance a spectator of the martyrdom of Jerome of Prague, and have witnessed there his complete intellectual helplessness. That was in 1416. Exactly a century later, and some sixty years after the death of Valla, there appeared at Froben's press in Basle Erasmus' edition of the Greek Testament. The history of this book presents many paradoxes. Erasmus, in the course of twenty years, gave to the press five editions of it. But there were printed during his lifetime without his authority between sixty and seventy editions.

If he was injured in this, or his printers injured, unknowingly he had himself injured a grand rival. For this *editio princeps* of the Greek Testament is, we know, not *editio* vere *princeps*. More than two years before, the Spanish printer Brocario had put *finis* to the noble edition of the New Testament, Greek and Latin, commissioned by Cardinal Ximenes. But Ximenes' great Bible, begun in 1502, was not licensed for publication until 1520. Erasmus' Greek Testament, by accident the first, thereafter for a period of more than three hundred years looked very like being the last. Stephanus' text of 1550 was, in essentials, a reprint of Erasmus' edition of 1535. In this country, it became, and continued to be till 1881, the *textus receptus*. Until 1881 an Englishman reading the New Testament read it in a version which rendered the Greek text of Erasmus; a text notable for the circumstance that, in the last five verses of the Book of Revelation, Erasmus, having only a defective Greek manuscript,[1] supplied the Greek himself by translation from the Latin. In 1707 Mills listed, from the MSS. known to him, some 30,000 variants from this 'received text'. Like Erasmus,

[1] It belonged to Reuchlin. Erasmus thought it so old that it might have been written in the Apostolic Age (note on *Apoc.* 3, 7). Palaeographers who have examined it assign it to the twelfth century.

he was assailed for tampering with the Word of God. He was defended by Bentley.

Other paradoxes of this book I will touch only lightly. One of the decisive books of the world, it comes to us from the most undeciding of men. Luther and the Pope, the Gospel and the World, Truth and Equivocation—these sharp antitheses hurt Erasmus. Yet this book not only made Luther, for the first time it made the Gospel intelligible, everywhere for what is worse than untruth, obscurantism, substituting the grace and truth of good sense. Parts of it have the quality, it may be, less of scholarship than of some supremely inspired journalism. The prefatory Address to the Reader, the so-called *Paraclesis*, must be read always, if only for the sentences in which Erasmus forecasts a vernacular New Testament which shall be music in the mouth of the countryman driving his plough, the weaver plying his shuttle, the wayfaring man dragging weary feet. To those sentences, we may believe, the world owes Luther's Bible and the New Testament of Tindale. The *Novum Instrumentum* of 1516, meantime, could reach only lettered readers, clerks who had Latin, however bad. In the *Apologia* prefixed to it, 'God does not much mind bad grammar', Erasmus tells them, 'but he does not take any particular pleasure in it—*at idem non delectatur*'. God has delivered the Gospel to us in some four thousand different Greek MSS. —of which Erasmus knew (in 1516) five. In addition there are some eight thousand Latin MSS. Not one text agrees with the other. In this respect the MSS. of the Scriptures are like those of secular writings. To discover what an evangelist wrote, what an apostle wrote, there is required a method of scholarship not different from that by which we try to find what Homer or Virgil wrote. It is the immortal achievement of Erasmus that in his Greek Testament he broke down for good and all the barrier between sacred and profane learning. The age-long battle of scholarship with the Church had been joined in earnest: what Valla had done was but a preliminary skirmish. The principles of humanism had been carried triumphantly into the region of sacred literature. Before the conclusions of his own premisses, indeed, Erasmus stands timid and astonished. To the more daring and eager spirits he seemed a lost leader; it was as though he had occupied a position for the purpose of evacuating it.

Between Erasmus and Scaliger lie the Reformation and the French wars of religion. 'All religious differences', Scaliger once said, 'proceed from want of scholarship—*ab ignoratione grammaticae*.' The spirit of that utterance is the spirit which animates the two masterpieces of his scholarship, the *Emendatio Temporum* and the *Thesaurus Temporum*. In the Prolegomena to the *Thesaurus* he speaks in solemn terms of a scholarship which is the study of truth, and of truth as one whether in religious or secular inquiries. He speaks as one who has carried into unattempted regions a victorious crusade. Of his earlier work in scholarship I have not space to speak here. Most of it had been concerned with the criticism of texts. Suffice it to say that in his editions of Festus, the minor Virgilian poems, the Latin elegists, and Manilius, he laid anew the foundations of an art, or science, which has always held a high place among the occupations of scholarship. He introduced principle where before whim had reigned. He made conjecture dependent upon a clear understanding of an author's meaning. He set the example of a scholar who put the love of truth above the display of mere ingenuity. These early works were accomplished amid the distractions of the Huguenot wars—distractions, he tells Pithou, which had well-nigh killed his edition of the Virgilian *opuscula*. These works, no doubt, suffered something from a necessary discontinuity in their execution. They may have gained something also in directness and reality from the conditions out of which they arose. But it was with the *Emendatio*

Temporum that Scaliger first captured the ear of Europe. Till then, his fame was provincial. Not the essentials of the book, however, but an accident of religious politics, brought him this extended repute. In 1582 a Bull of Pope Gregory XIII imposed the Lilian Calendar on the Catholic world. It was adopted at once in Italy, Spain and Portugal; and accepted after a two-months delay by the Parliament of France. In the spring of the year following appeared Scaliger's *Emendatio Temporum*, dedicated to the President of the Parliament—Harlay, who was known to look with disfavour on the New Calendar. Two sections of the book treated of the Lilian Year; some of the points made by Scaliger against Lilius are said by astronomers to have force. But the Calendar was, in many of the states of Europe, a part of politics. Whatever conveniences the Lilian Year had, it had the inconvenience that it was dictated from Rome. And so it was that the *Emendatio* found for Scaliger a wider public than any he had hitherto known. It was a public which he retained to the end; a public made aware by accident of a learning the like of which had never been known. Nearly a quarter of a century later, Scaliger published the *Thesaurus Temporum*, the grand sequel to the *Emendatio*. The *Thesaurus* is probably the most learned book in the world.

Nobody now reads either of these great books; nor, perhaps, needs to. And for a reason ever so simple. The learning of them has become long since a part of the common stock of scholarship. We use it in all our studies as we use air and the light, with little thought of the genius which built the firmament and divided the darkness from the day. This penalty follows, indeed, all consummate work, all achievement that is fundamental. Such work, in the words of Scaliger's favourite poet,

fundamenta tenet rerum...
Effectu minor in specie, sed maior in usu.

The two books constitute together a treatise upon chronology. But they are a great deal more than that. What arrests us at once is their infinite outlook. Merely turning the leaves of the *Emendatio*, glancing at the Tables, the reader becomes aware that Scaliger is a scholar in not less than seven ancient tongues. In the Latin tongue he was plainly the greatest scholar the world had produced. In the Greek tongue he was second only to Casaubon, whose fame was junior. But he was a scholar also—not so good a scholar, it is said, but a scholar—in Hebrew, in Arabic, in Ethiopic, in Syriac, in Persian. So equipped, he altered for ever the whole horizon of learning.

Beholding in one equal view east and west, he brought into the world—he, first of men—the conception of the unity of history. The ancient world could be understood only as a whole. Greece and Rome could not be understood in separation from Egypt and the East; nor biblical history without the aid of secular learning. A harmony of ancient history had been essayed in the fourth century by Eusebius. What was known of the Chronicle of Eusebius existed only in Jerome's abridgement of the second book of it. This Latin Eusebius Scaliger made the basis of his reconstruction of ancient history. Studying it, he divined that there was a lost first book. His recovery of this lost book may be accounted the most extraordinary feat of learning ever achieved. Into the detail of it I cannot here enter. In one particular Scaliger was notably assisted by fortune; which supplied to him from the Royal Library in Paris a MS. of the ninth-century chronicler Syncellus. 'Truly I can say', Scaliger writes to a Cambridge scholar, Richard Thomson, 'that I have raised Eusebius from the dead.' In the *Thesaurus* he gives a complete Eusebius, his own restoration, his own Greek. Round it he assembles every known scrap of Greek and Latin chronological writing, making his texts intelligible by emendation and comment. In 1881 there was printed in Venice, from a twelfth-century Armenian MS., the Chronicle of Eusebius perfect in all its parts. In a good many particulars it did not confirm Scaliger's restoration. But the main outline it left standing. The lost first book was there. It did not contain all that Scaliger had conjecturally assigned to it. But the Armenian version left his book fairly entitled to be called one of the great miracles of critical divination.

Scaliger was not a great teacher; he was not, as Politian was, born for the classroom—indeed, he hated teaching. When he succeeded Lipsius at Leiden, it was part of the bargain that he should lecture or not, as he liked. All that Leiden asked was that he should be there. The mere neighbourhood of this princely learning was enough. Something too much of the princely, perhaps, his learning sometimes carried. Yet he gave his friendship freely to young men. To such men as Daniel Heinsius, Grotius, John Dousa, John Rutgers, to the compilers of the second *Scaligerana*, and others, his hearth was free; and there radiated from it the pure enthusiasm of literature. His literary judgements—to his contemporaries they were rather 'dooms' than criticisms—have been collected together by an American scholar, Mr G. W. Robinson,[1] and repay study. Dogmatic

[1] *Harvard Studies in Classical Philology*, xxix, 1918.

and unconventional, they are always arresting and stimulating; where they traverse accepted opinion they bear the stamp of an unbribed judgement. If his Letters have less of entertaining quality, they are the letters, even so, of a princely scholar. He supposed it to be possible to be a poet in Greek and Latin. He did not think himself so good a poet as his father, the most voluminous of versifiers; whether he was right or wrong does not matter.

Scaliger was hardly dead when there set in a marked decline in the repute of scholarship. More causes than one contributed to bring about this diminution of prestige. The principal of these I have already noticed—already in Scaliger's lifetime the languages and literatures of modern Europe were asserting themselves decisively against those of antiquity; the same force, namely patriotism, which in Italy had given birth to classical studies was now, outside Italy, threatening their security. The disruption of the Catholic Church contributed to the same end. While the Roman Church stood entire Latin was necessarily cultivated as the only means of intercommunication which the different members of it possessed.[1] It now became in the nature of things less essential.

[1] In this connexion Valla, *Oratio in Principio Sui Studii*, is worth consulting.

It is obvious also that the disputes within the Church had for a long time kept the attention of the world fixed upon documents written in the ancient tongues, and that the adjustment of these disputes must necessarily cause this attention to be sensibly relaxed. The dissemination of the Bible in the vernacular tongues worked in the same direction. Everywhere the conditions were preparing which were to make scholarship and the study of literature no longer synonymous. In particular we must not forget that the profession of the scholar had owed its importance hitherto to the fact that the ancient writers had been regarded not merely as the masters of thought and language but as the masters of knowledge. Here is a consideration so obvious that we are apt to overlook it. Dante had spoken of Aristotle as the 'master of them that *know*'. To-day the student does not go to Aristotle to learn natural history, to Hippocrates or to Galen to learn medicine, nor to Ptolemy for his astronomy. But Bacon, Harvey, Galileo were all of them younger than Scaliger; and it was only with them that the ancient writers ceased to be regarded as the sources of scientific knowledge.

It was in the nature of things, therefore, that the repute of scholarship should, precisely from the moment when in Scaliger it reached its culmination, begin to decline. We may even say that the character itself of Scaliger's greatness assisted this decline. It was Scaliger more than any other scholar who brought into scholarship the spirit of science. It is the characteristic of this spirit that it so often girds us and carries us whither we would not. It carries us from the simple to the complex, and from that to a yet greater complexity; until presently it is impossible for a single mind to compass the multifarious subject-matter presented. Hence comes what is called specialism, and a learning of partial effects, wanting, often, imaginative quality.

The scholar who, among those who followed Scaliger, may be thought likest Scaliger in his scholarship, is perhaps Bentley. We have noticed already in passing that Bentley's greatest work, the *Letters of Phalaris*, was written, not in Latin, but in English. We have noticed how out of that work arose Swift's *Battle of the Books*. Swift's Satire puts considerations of which to-day some, I fancy, are still ponderable. That the services of the scholar to European thought have been in the past immense, no one will deny. It was he who vindicated for the imaginative reason its place in life. It was he who recast our ideal of the education of the human race. It was he who gave to the world the conception of universal history, and the ideal of the unity of learning. It was he who carried liberty of thought into the sphere of religion, into a sphere, that is, where, from the very grandeur of the issues involved, such liberty is more than anywhere else salutary, and indeed essential. It was he, once again, and not the scientist, who first brought into study the spirit of science. When we turn from the contemplation of these great services in the past, to consider what the scholar is doing to-day, and what, if he were not doing that, he might be doing, I will not say *difficile est satiram non scribere*, I will not say that our scholarship invites satire. But it does, I think, put questions. If I find some of these disquieting, I feel it, none the less, to be in the spirit of scholarship to attend to them. Johnson and Bentley were impressed by the unhappiness of scholars. For myself, I have not seen much of it. Of scholars who came to the scaffold—*real* scholars, for I am so far with Macaulay that I cannot think of Laud as a scholar—I recall from history only one, Dolet. Nor in real life have I seen much of the unhappiness of scholars. I have known scholars who had few pleasures, scholars who never found preferment. But most of them—in part, I must think, because they sought neither pleasure nor preferment—have been happy. The real peril of the scholar, I would suggest, is not unhappiness, but that, too happy in his happiness, he asks no questions about it. It is a high price to pay for any kind of happiness, to have no metaphysic.

In 1892 Housman inaugurated his London professorship by a lecture, not on the uses—for he thought it had none—but on the value of classical learning. A great scholar and, as I shall always think, a great poet—if with a range somewhat limited and special—Housman had also—what I delight in scarcely less—a fine gift of slapdash journalism. His lecture begins gravely and happily. '"Every exercise of our faculties", says Aristotle, "has some good for its aim"; and if he speaks true it becomes a matter of importance that when we exercise any special faculty we should clearly apprehend the special good at which we are aiming. What now is the good which we set before us in acquiring knowledge, in learning?' 'The partisans of science', Housman goes on, 'define the end of education as the useful, the partisans of the Humanities define it, more sublimely, as the good and beautiful.' Housman has no use for partisans. The good of science is not the useful. Unless so far as it helps us to propel ships, the science of astronomy is about as useless as even science can be. Let our Newtons 'carry their Principias to some other market'. The good of classical scholarship, again, is not the good and the beautiful. 'The classics cannot be said to have succeeded altogether in transforming and beautifying Milton's inner nature. They did not sweeten his naturally disagreeable temper; they did not enable him to conduct controversy with urbanity or even with decency.' Something they did for his poetry. Even so, 'compare', says Housman, 'Shakespeare and Milton, and see what the classics did for the one and what the lack of classics did for the other'. From Milton he turns to Bentley. Bentley, like most of his contemporaries, 'brought with him into the world...a prosaic mind; nor did all his immense study of the classics avail to confer on him a true appreciation of poetry. While he dealt with the classical poets he was comparatively safe, for in dealing with these a prosaic mind is not so grave a disqualification as a dithyrambic mind; and Bentley had lived with the ancients till he understood them as no man will ever understand them who brings to their study a taste formed on the poetry of Elizabeth's time or ours.' Note the implications. We poor English, whose best in poetry is Shakespeare, we romantics, whose only supreme classical poet is Milton—Milton whose inner nature the classics so signally failed to beautify—if we wish to understand the ancients, we must change our taste, forgo or forget

Shakespeare and his crowd. If Bentley understood the classics, it was because his taste was not vitiated by the study of Shakespeare. You might expect him, so, to have understood Milton. But not a bit of it. His taste here is as bad as it could be. As a critic of Milton he has, Housman says, only one good quality, his 'intrepid candour'. 'There is a sort of savage nobility about his firm reliance on his own bad taste.' Of 'intrepid candour' Housman himself has a good deal. 'If a certain department of knowledge', he writes, 'attracts a man, let him study that, and study it because it attracts him, and let him not fabricate excuses.' Let us have no more talk about 'the best which has been said and thought in the world —the literature which contains the history of the spirit of man'. Textual criticism—so he comes to his own subject—'is one of the drier and less palpitating sciences'. That does not render it 'any less worthy of pursuit' than 'those sciences which, in Bacon's phrase, are drenched in flesh and blood.' If it attracts a man more than any other science, that is good enough. He may 'rest assured that the reason why it attracts him is that it s best for him'. Housman's 'central theme' in this lecture (says the Editor of it) is 'the value of learning for "its own sake"'. Rather, the central theme, I must believe, is that all learning is good, but any kind of learning is as good as another. It is as good as another, so far as a man can be happy with it.

It is a high price to pay for any kind of happiness—to have no metaphysic, or as little as this. I am not, in truth, quite sure whether, for Housman, scholarship is happiness; whether he does not conceive it rather as an anodyne, an anodyne for the wounds of life and disappointed talent. He spoke of his lecture as 'not wholly sincere'. It wants, I believe, sincerity. It wants also metaphysic. But above all, it wants history. It makes nonsense of five centuries of history. The scholars who recovered antiquity for us, the scholars who made the Reformation, the scholars who made Truth one—the same for men and for priests— Poggio, Valla, Politian, Erasmus, Scaliger—I have called up their ghosts for witness. These great ghosts, when they have answered our questioning, have questions of their own for us. They see us doing to-day, most of us, and calling it scholarship, very much what they were doing when it more wanted doing. Of our sedulous *imitatio veterum*, of the time and talent that we give to Greek and Latin composition, what causes, if they question us, shall we allege? Is this just a tradition which we have accepted unthinkingly from a time when no modern language was an adequate vehicle of classical expression? Our textual criticism, again, our endless apparatus of conjectural emendation, about that too can we satisfy their wonder? for wonder and astonishment there may well be with them when they see us lavishing on fair and generally intelligible texts much the same pains as were imposed on themselves by texts corrupt and disordered. Of these and other exercises of our scholarship the fascination cannot be denied; nor that they demand for their successful prosecution a very high order of gifts. But they do not stand outside question. The Renaissance, that second birth of the world, is past history. In this second death of the world, which is the times in which we live, can these ancient luxuries of our scholarship stay with us? Or shall we have taken from us first these our loved pedantries, and anon the grand causes of them, the humanities, the genialities, poetry, rhetoric, and the freedom of question and answer?

If I knew the answer to this question, I should perhaps not ask it. I will play at question and answer in a final lecture. But I will try to be brief, and I undertake to be inconclusive.

III

I TAKE leave to begin my last lecture with something which belonged more properly, perhaps, to my first—a string of excuses. When I was invited by the Cambridge Faculty Board of Classics to give these lectures on the Gray foundation, so great a compliment pleased me mightily, but was not wanting in embarrassment. In accepting the invitation, I felt something of a pretender, and said so. But it was not thought to matter; any Oxford man, perhaps, lecturing in Cambridge *must* be something of a pretender—if only for the sake of Oxford, he must pretend to be better than he is. I was only one of a long procession— Erasmus, teaching in Cambridge the Greek he failed to learn in Oxford, begins it. I say that, and know that I should not, but that I should remember Erasmus only in noble connexions. I spoke of his Greek Testament as one of the decisive books of the world, saying something, though not enough, of its place in the history of scholarship. After his Greek Testament, his greatest book, his most living monument, is his Letters. Literature has not such another picture of the life of scholarship, of the ills that assail the scholar's life, and of its grand consolations. It is pleasant to me to recall that this Gray lectureship commemorates a scholar who practised scholarship in Erasmus' college of Queens'. Just two hundred and fifty years ago the Letters of Erasmus were edited by the Leiden professor Leclerc, a Swiss Arminian, but one of the benefactors of mankind, though he had the misfortune to be a good deal bullied by Bentley. A new edition of them was undertaken at the beginning of this century by P. S. Allen. Bywater called Allen 'the most learned man in Oxford'; and I think he was, except for Bywater himself. Allen lived to finish eight only of the eleven volumes of his edition. The task of editing the last three volumes he bequeathed to Mrs Allen and myself; and except that we are still struggling with the proofs of the final volume, the task is discharged. I mention this because for twelve years Erasmus has been my only direct connexion with scholarship. Once I had closer connexions. For three-and-twenty years I taught classics. To-day, I am but a pensioner of the classics. When I was asked to give these lectures, I wrote, speaking truth, that I was in some sense a runagate of the classics.

The efficiency of teaching depends upon faith. After the first great War, the War of 1914–18, like the rest of the world, I lost faith in a good many things. To-day, of course, I could almost count on my fingers the things that I have not lost faith in. After 1918, I seemed to detect in myself a certain loss of faith in the classics, in the classics as taught. I still took pleasure in textual criticism and composition—from the fifteenth century until now the staple of classical teaching. I took pleasure in them myself—I still do: custom does not wither nor time wasted stale the infinite fascination of them. But I began to doubt the *morality* of them. For their successful prosecution they require, I have said, a high order of gifts—a very high order of gifts. Most students want these gifts, or are not interested to have them. Nor could I but ask myself whether those who have them might not better employ gifts of such quality elsewhere. I will not labour misgivings which I have already hinted—I will not ask why, here and in so much of our scholarship, we still stand where the first scholars stood. In connexion, however, with our *imitatio veterum*, I will hazard an observation which I think timely. I hate it that the practice of Latin composition should be allowed to dominate still, as it does, the department of elegy and sepulchral inscription. Our dead of the first Great War, the nearer and dearer dead of this last and greater one, must they, in our schools and colleges, for their best honour lie lapped in Latin? Is our English not tender enough, or not hard enough, for these offices of pride, grief, gratitude? I know that I have Dr Johnson against me. I know, too, for these purposes what fine effects the Latin keeps. All our best epitaphs are the Latin ones; hitherto, in comparison, our English has failed us. But are we for ever to accept defeat? I do not like to believe, I do not believe, that English can never do this last piety. It never can if we will not give it a chance, expecting failures at first, and then more failures, but presently success and ease of spirit.

Just the other day—and because of the War, and our toll of dead—Mr John Sparrow made a collection of the best sepulchral inscriptions in Latin furnished by English churches and books. *Lapidaria*, a beautiful book—for it was produced by the Cambridge University Press, under the direction of Mr Stanley Morison—a collector's book, lovely in its luxury, it was printed privately, so that a man can neither buy it, nor, if he might, afford to. Looking at it with impotent longing, what a challenge, I felt, such a book was, now especially, to our pride of English. It had only the best. But how unbeatable! How unbeatable, in a single example, something we all know, the Wren epitaph in St Paul's: *Si monumentum requiris, circumspice*. English will not easily beat that solemn beauty of epigram. But the challenge of its perfection is there, for us to take up. May I suggest here that Dyer, Lamb's friend, the historian of the Cambridge colleges, did not too badly by Wren in an English sentence? Speaking of the Library of Trinity, 'Here it was', he writes, 'that our great master of Palladian architecture, Sir Christopher Wren, surveyed his own work, and was satisfied.' Dyer was not making an inscription for the façade of the Trinity Library. This fine sentence fell from him as by accident; yet admonishing us, I feel, that, for commemorating greatness briefly, English can do something.

A little earlier, but similarly during the War, Mr Sparrow gave us two other anthologies: two booklets of Latin poetry written by Englishmen. Not Latin verse, but Latin poetry: professedly, that law governed Mr Sparrow's selection, and he obeyed it, I think, fairly. Latin poetry, the thing can still be done. Once or twice, two centuries ago, Gray of Peterhouse did it:

> *O lachrymarum fons tenero sacros...*

Mr Sparrow has that of course. But he comes down to our own day; and with decisive effects:

> *En cape: nos populo uenit inlatura perempto*
> *ossa solo quae det dissoluenda dies*
> *fataque sortitas non immortalia mentes*
> *et non aeterni uincla sodalicii.*

That is Housman; in a poem which someone somewhere has called his best and truest. But that is nonsense. Yet poetry this Latin piece is. I cannot forbear adding that in Mr Sparrow's booklets I first made acquaintance with the poems of the Master of Magdalene: βαιὰ μὲν ἀλλὰ ῥόδα: poems few but roses. But let me emphasize that these anthologies *are* booklets, not books. If Mr Sparrow ran to a third booklet, verily I believe he would run out of poetry into verse. He would run into that kind of accomplishment which I think not worth while in this after-the-war world; a world dying for want of poetry.

For our *imitatio veterum*, so much may suffice; very likely, you will think it more than enough. About our textual criticism I have said already, by implication, most of what I am concerned to say. That the textual critic is the happiest of men, and that that is enough—not even from Housman can I take that. In general, though something, no doubt, depends on the text, textual criticism is, for its practitioners, good fun. In the fifteenth century, it was both good fun and good sense. It was good sense, and it was necessary, because texts were bad. Often, it was both good sense and piety; for everywhere scholarship had to contend with religious imposture. To-day, how many Greek and Latin books are there, worth our

study, of which we have not texts good enough
for salvation? What may be added is for ornament
and curiosity. How safe we are to-day from
imposture, both secular and religious, we forget.
Erasmus' Greek Testament was, as a work of
scholarship, singularly imperfect. In 1516 he built
his text on MSS. of no account, none of them
earlier than the twelfth century. In 1521, and
again in 1534, his attention was called to the great
Codex Vaticanus. That it was written in the uncial
character meant nothing to him. Where it agrees
with the Vulgate of Jerome, against his own late
and worthless MSS., he supposes the text of it to
have been accommodated to the Latin at some
date later than 1435. This precious nonsense he
communicates gravely to a friend of the Spanish
scholar Stunica.[1] Stunica was one of the editors
of the great Alcala edition of the Bible, the so-
called Complutensian Polyglot. The Complutensian Greek Testament was, in everything except
date of publication, prior to that of Erasmus: and,
if truth be told, better scholarship went to it. But
one thing Erasmus had which the Alcala editors
had not, liberty of mind. The Alcala editors give
the whole Bible. In respect of the Old Testament,
they apologize for printing the Greek text, the

[1] Epp. 2938 (Allen). For Erasmus' inability to date MSS.
see p. 38, note.

Septuagint. In a central column they place the Vulgate, with the Hebrew text upon the one side, and on the other the Greek; patterning, they dare say, Christ crucified—for he hung between two thieves. Recently, a fine scholar, a priest of the Roman Church, a man of genius, an Oxford man, has published a new English version of the Vulgate New Testament. Behind this ingenious undertaking are the critical presuppositions of the Complutensian Polyglot and the Council of Trent. The true text of the New Testament, that is, is the Latin text. St Paul wrote in Greek. But if you wish to know what he wrote, where it is at all doubtful, you must go to Jerome's Latin—and Monsignor Knox's English. To-day, to most of us, this seems absurd. Monsignor Knox himself, I suspect, is not too happy about it. But to none of us, now, does it matter. It can no longer do any harm. We have found safety, long since: safety by a path made open to us by the fearless feet of Valla and the fearful feet of Erasmus.

The mention of the Complutensian Polyglot may excuse me here for recalling to your thoughts an ideal of sixteenth-century scholarship, present always to the mind of Erasmus, and a part purpose with the founders of some of our colleges, the ideal of the three tongues. Our best scholarship is still two-tongued, the Hebrew wanting. Till the other day, of course, though we forget it, all scholarship was primarily the business of the clergy. A learned laity, learned above the merely gentlemanly, is a modernism. That this lay learning should be two-tongued might have been expected; it might have been expected even if the clerical learning which it dispossessed had been—what, except in a few examples, it was not—three-tongued. Attending at one time daily the chapel services of my college, I liked to follow the Lesson for the day with the Septuagint version open in front of me; occasionally, I followed it with the Vulgate: the miscellaneous literature in my pew afforded opportunity for both exercises. 'Man is born unto trouble as the sparks fly upwards.' So the English, and, to the same effect, I supposed, the Hebrew. But 'Man is born unto trouble, and the bird for flying', the Vulgate has it—*homo nascitur ad laborem, et avis ad volatum.* And yet again, 'Man is born to trouble, but the young of a vulture fly in the heights', says the Septuagint; till I do not know where I am. Nor am I much better off when, from the margin of the Revised Version, I learn that the Hebrew gives, not what the Revised Version gives, but, for the 'sparks' or bird or vulture's young, it gives 'the sons of flame', or 'the sons of lightning'. These variants do not involve salvation. But the book of Job *matters*; and the three tongues are wanted for it. Nor do I know when salvation itself may not be involved. Righteousness matters; and I meet it up and down the Old Testament. I know that it does not always there mean the same thing. But I do not know that it ever means what I mean. I know that the Greek word ἀρετή, commonly rendered by 'virtue', does not mean, nine times out of ten, what you and I mean by virtue. But I have no check upon 'righteousness'. The righteous man, for all I know, may not be all that different from the nice man; and I await with curious complacency a commentary telling me that righteousness is good sense, or even the art of getting on in the world. I remember with what a shock it came to me, years back, to be told, in a celebrated French commentary, that in 'Remember now thy creator in the days of thy youth' the first four words should properly be rendered 'Remember now the pleasures of love'. It fits in so well—'or ever the evil days come, or the years draw nigh when thou shalt say, I have no pleasure in them'. It fits in ever so well. But I am told that it is wrong, and must believe what I am told. If I could start my scholarship all over again, I would have nothing to do with Greek and Latin composition, nor remember any more the pleasures of conjectural emendation. But give me, I would say, the three tongues.

As it is, my three tongues must be, for scholarship, the Greek, the Latin and my own. For my own has now its own scholarship; the interest of it competing powerfully in our schools with that of Greek and Latin. And it is with this in mind that I turn to that department of classical learning and teaching which consists in literary and historical criticism.

Here too I feel myself not wholly outside the region of moral doubt. That a man could hardly be better employed than in interesting students in the best of Greek and Latin literature, I have never doubted. I would even put in a plea for the second best and third best. Too selective, I mean, we live too much with scraps of antiquity. But I will not labour this. Till we have more time, let us put up with the best. I am anxious only that we should deal with the best honestly; and I wonder sometimes whether too many of us do not spend too much of our time making the classics interesting by saying things about them that are not true. Particularly does this happen, I fancy, in connexion with Greek literature. For to do it there is so easy. And in what follows I will confine myself to Greek literature.

In 1918, Greek was, as it always is, dying. That it had been hit badly by the Great War is possible. Immediately after the War, in Oxford it ceased to be compulsory in the entrance examinations to the University. The meaning of this was plain, at any rate to a good many of my friends. It had been secretly stabbed in the back by domestic enemies. Much as a man hates to vote against his bread and butter, I recall with satisfaction that I registered an honest man's vote against the retention of Greek as a compulsory subject. Greek is still dying. I fear less that it will actually do so than that, in our efforts to save it, we may be betrayed into bearing false witness. We *do* commonly, I think, say about it a good many things that are not true. We do so, I fancy, from a wish to persuade the student of the modern literatures that in the ancient, in the Greek before all, there is something to miss which is to miss everything. Some of the things which we say let me list.

First, I think it not true to say that the classical is really romantic. It makes it more interesting, I know—for we are all romantics at heart. Yet it is just not true. But, in effect, it is for ever being said. It is hardly permitted, indeed, now to distinguish classical and romantic at all.

It seems to me, again, not true to call the Greek drama drama. It seems to me truer to call it, say, statuary, than to drag it into the same literary kind as Shakespeare. It is a different kind—a kind which I have no wish to disparage. Yet if anyone tells me that he does not know whether the *Oedipus* or *Hamlet* be the greater work of human imagination, frankly, I do not believe him, or I cease to respect him. About the Greek drama in itself, I will add, I feel still a fundamental disquiet. It seems to me a never properly adjusted fusion between two elements which, for convenience, I will call the Attic and the Doric. When I was a boy in one of the lower forms at school, we used to read the dialogue parts (for they were Attic) and leave out the choruses—they were too hard. Now I read the choruses and leave out the rest; and I await the day when somebody will have the courage to say that the Greek drama was spoiled by becoming Attic. People have complained of Gilbert Murray for rendering the non-choric portions of Greek tragedy by rhymed verse. But here, though not everywhere perhaps, he knew what he was doing. The rhymed decasyllabic couplets are wanted; for the original has the same jejunity as Pope.

I am going to let the flood of heretical opinion carry me yet further. For the purpose of composition, of the *imitatio veterum*, our reading in Greek—I speak of Oxford custom—is directed above all upon the Attic writers, prose and verse. When I taught Greek, I could not tell my pupils that these were the worst parts of Greek literature —that the fifth century B.C. marked (except for Plato) a progressive degeneration of language and style. I could not say *that*, but I believed it. Plato stands in his own circle of light; and the mystery of him—why he is not Attic—I have not the learning to penetrate. But when I read, first Homer, and then Pindar and the great lyrists, and then Herodotus (I think they are still my favourite Greek authors), when, after reading these, I turn to the Attics, I feel myself in a world comparatively mean and in parts of it dowdy. Atticism and the Attic—whether ancient or modern—I believe that in the heart of us we all hate it, or are all a little bored with it, and dare not say so.

I have set Plato on a throne by himself. I can bring myself to say no harm of him. Yet in a sense he has fooled us beyond any of the Greeks. He has taught us to think of the Greeks as though they were all of them Platos. He has diffused a curious cant about everything Hellenic: a cant which I have talked myself, and which I listen to now with impatience from others. I suppose that nine persons out of ten of those who are superficially interested in things Hellenic

would, if they were asked what the world owed
to Greece, discover it in the circumstance that the
Greeks were, before all else, lovers of the beautiful.
I should be the tenth person. While not challenging the power with which the Greeks developed
and illustrated a special, a specially Greek, conception of the beautiful, I should, none the less, be
disposed to contend, first, that this rather special
conception has influenced the modern world far
less than we pretend, and secondly, that, though
we rightly emphasize the addiction of the Greeks
to the idea of beauty, our most real debt to them
lies, not there, but elsewhere. When we emphasize
the Greek love of beauty, we emphasize, of course,
that side of the Greek spirit which is most engaging
and attaching; and that is why we do so. It is
easy here to say interesting things about them. It
is dull—and I admit it—it is dull to praise them
for what I none the less feel to be that quality of
their spirit which makes them a race apart—for
the logicality and honesty of their minds. Take
the Eastern literatures—or take even the Gothic
literatures. In the former there is a good deal of
thinking. Do we not feel the thinking of these
literatures to be done in a different kind, and even
with a different kind of instrument, from that to
which we are accustomed? We are accustomed
to what we have received; and we have received

it from the Greeks. I do not mean, of course, that the Greeks first formulated for us what we call the laws of logic—a very doubtful benefit, in any case. I mean rather that they were the first to bring pure rationality into use, the first people to exhibit complete intellectual honesty, to try to see things as they are, and to state them plainly, to get things down to their lowest terms.

That I am not thinking of any narrow *mere* logicality, let me indicate by two illustrations.

In the nineteenth book of the *Iliad*, Homer presents Briseis and her women, weeping over the death of Patroclus. He gives us at length the words of Briseis' Lament; and then he adds: 'Thus spake she weeping, and her women added to her lament their own. They pretended to lament Patroclus, but each of them in fact lamented her own woes.' They were captive women; and Homer sacrifices poetry to honesty; for to tell the truth here, thus barely, was not, for poetry, wanted: the beauty of the context is, to modern feeling, sensibly injured.

In the first book of the *Ethics*, Aristotle, considering the nature of Happiness, raises the question whether Happiness, whether the highest life, human self-realization, is possible for someone who has the misfortune to be utterly ugly (πaναισχής). Most of us, given such a question, would shilly-shally. Might not the very ugly, perhaps, be blessed in very much the same way as the poor? But Aristotle knows that the utterly ugly man does not get on in the world, does not get what he wants, is precluded from full self-realization; and he says so plainly.

That second illustration I value enormously. What Aristotle says there everybody knows to be true. But who else—what moralist, what man—dare say it? We live, most of us, by preference, with shams—we like above all those shams which tend to glorify human nature.

That this divine candour of the Greek spirit, this logical disinterestedness, has its perils, I would not deny—the border-line is narrow which divides complete intellectual honesty from cynicism. What I am set to urge, however, is that in our different renaissances, in the various returns which from time to time the human spirit has made upon Greek ideas, in all our Greek studies, in fact, no gain has been—no gain is—quite commensurate with that which we derive from Greek logicality, Greek sincerity, Greek good sense. The truth is that it is much easier to love the beautiful than to love the true, or the sensible. The Greeks did both. But while we are still behind them in fearlessness of logic, in moral and intellectual frankness—and also, I might perhaps add, in the clearness of our political thinking—we have gone far beyond them (I have no doubt at all) in our aesthetic. We have made a better success of the beautiful; to some extent, it may be, from our comparative defect of logic. The Greek too much carried his logicality into his conception of the beautiful, too much circumscribing beauty by the ideas of symmetry, proportion, harmony. He will never allow the beautiful to run wild, he will never indulge it with depth and mystery.

A bias towards this more indulgent treatment of it may, I should suppose, be discerned in Plato. Even so, what is more plainly discerned is Plato's fear of it in himself. We have too much inferred from Plato that the dominant quality of the Greek spirit is the love of beauty. Yet how nervous Plato is about the beautiful! How he would like it to be mathematics!

The average Greek, I must think, was about as little like Plato as the average Englishman is like, let me say, Keats. But it makes the Greek spirit interesting to make all Greeks like Plato, and Plato like Keats. Yet all the while we do it, we are endangering our intellectual honesty. At least I like to remind myself from time to time that the Greeks are pre-eminently the masters of good sense. I regret that they too much carried good sense into their conception of the beautiful.

What does our own literature owe, what ought it to owe, to the Greek? Much every way, as St Paul says. But I think it desirable even here to avoid exaggeration. For the critical study of any of the great modern literatures, for a scholar's study of them, a knowledge of Greek literature is, I feel, indispensable; and what is wanted can hardly be supplied by translations. Greek literature is the best commentary we can have upon almost any other literature. Its *critical* value is immense. On the other hand, for a writer, be he poet or proser, who wishes to do creative work, the best way to be a Greek, I have always thought, is not to try to be one. That is an honest and Greek way of looking at things. The most Greek effects in our literature have not come from the conscious study of Greek models.

I am led so to say something about the scholarship of translation. Of the work of the Renaissance scholars in this kind, the early Latin renderings from the Greek, I have no first-hand knowledge. The first great practitioner here was Leonardus Brunus; and a landmark is Valla's Thucydides.[1] I shall concern myself only with renderings which employ the vernacular. I sometimes wonder

[1] Poggio made a Latin translation of the *Cyropaedia*. Of his Latin, his son Jacopo printed an Italian version, Florence, 1521.

whether anybody ever reads the Greek Testament for pleasure, pleasure in the Greek. For myself, I have never met anyone who did, not so much as a clergyman. Just as literature, and for mere language, the English is better, the German is better. Tindale, you may say, translated the New Testament so well because he was rather like an apostle or an evangelist. That certainly might help. But I can think of a more obvious reason. If Tindale is better than his original, that, I suggest, may mean not much more than that he disposed a better language, his sixteenth-century English, a better language than the Hellenistic Greek. From the New Testament I should infer, for the theory of translation, no more than that a translation made in a good language from an original made in an inferior language is likely to be better worth reading than the original. I find the Greek of Plutarch difficult, the style unpleasing. I read the *Lives*, accordingly, in North, contentedly. If there were a good translation of the *Moralia*, or of the *Apophthegmata*—neglected books, crowded with ancient wisdom and greatness of action—I should never look again at the Greek. But when we pass to the great Greek classics, to the books written before the Greek language fell away from its supremacy of beauty, it is a different story. For it is plain truth—there is no getting away from it—

that of no one of the great Greek classics have we an adequate rendering; but our best is only second best. It is true even for prose. All our best is second best. Jowett is not like Plato; Jowett is not like Thucydides. What is worse, Plato and Thucydides—so unlike in their style, in the Greek—are very like one another in Jowett; both employ there the same moderately good style, and forfeit individual quality. I do not know that, translated by Jowett, they are very much like Jowett either; for outside translation, Jowett is (though nobody knows it, the anthologists have missed him) a great master of style—of the simple style an incomparable master. Herodotus, again—that nobody has rendered him adequately would matter less if it were possible to divine even dimly some craft by which he *might* be rendered: the dialect, the archaism, the naïve quality of the style, the liquidity of language, Ionian vowels voicing the soft Ionian melancholy of temper; without some utterly studied style, without unbearable affectation, without a hurting ingenuity, how shall anyone essay it, or, essaying it, remain readable?

If it is as bad as all that with the prose-writers, what shall a man say when he comes to our Englishing of the Greek poets?

And like a star upon her bosom lay
His beautiful and shining golden head.

Will any of you tell me (unless he knows already) what Greek poet those two fine lines English, or who the translator is? The poet translated is Homer (but how much more like Virgil the verse is!), and the poet translating him—here, for once in his life, once only, a poet, is Thomas Hobbes.[1] *And there is that Leviathan!*

No one has written a sonnet 'On first looking into Hobbes' Homer'. Keats' sonnet 'On first looking into Chapman's Homer' put the world out of love with the Homer of Pope; and if we read Chapman, it is, not for Chapman, but for Keats. Not but what one day, perhaps, when Chapman's Homer has fallen upon final neglect, chance or some lonely zeal of scholarship will rescue into immortality, as a supreme example of studied prose-rhythm, the last cadences of Chapman's Preface to the Hymns of Homer: Hear Homer, he says, in his Hymns: it is the same Homer still. 'Hear our ever the same intranced and never sleeping Master of the Muses to his last accent incomparably singing.' What compelling words of invitation! But the incomparable singing of Homer no genius of prose nor verse can

[1] See Clough, *Letters of Parepidemus II* (Prose Works, 1888, p. 390): 'How that first of English prosaists', says Clough, 'was inspired with [these two lines] remains a problem to all generations.'

English for us. The Master of the Muses must be music only for the scholar, the Grecian. Just the Greek words, and the movement of the Greek verse: just these reach only Grecian ears, and it is no good pretending. Of some classes of Greek verse the modern tongues can reproduce something like the pattern; in particular of that class of verse which I think the least to be esteemed, the iambic dodecasyllable. But Homer, and the great lyrists, and the measures of elegy—making poetry, these last, even of the verse of the Greek decadence, so that the Greek Anthology enshrines effects for ever moving and memorable—of these rhythms and metres it is not in the power of any modern tongue to give so much as a faint similitude.

That is why I will not raise a question often debated: Shall the translator of Greek poetry—of Homer, say—use verse or prose? From prose we shall suppose ourselves to get the *sense*, as it is called—uncomfortably aware that in poetry, very often, it is the last thing that we want. Soul and sound we shall miss, two effects the more valuable because they are, in truth, one. If, on the other hand, our translator uses verse, first, it will be a different verse. Think of Pope. Could the wit of man devise any measure less like the Greek hexameter, unless it were the English hexameter?

Secondly, if he gives us poetry, the chances are—though they are against any poetry at all—that it will be a different poetry from that of the original. I shall never persuade myself that Gilbert Murray is, except in his politics, really like Euripides. Likeness there should be, for Nature made Euripides for a professor. Where Murray is most a poet, he is, I always feel, least like Euripides. But I learned to hate Euripides, I admit, when I was very young. The poetry of Murray, his renderings of the choric measures of Greek drama, I learned to admire about the same time that I learned to admire Swinburne—and for the same sort of reasons. Murray and Euripides are, in any case, poets in a quite different kind. You could never guess the one from the other, any more than you could guess Homer from Pope.

To the aspirant after Greek, then, the 'young enthusiast' standing doubtfully between the choice of Greek and something else, pausing awhile from letters to be wise, I will not say, if he refuses Greek studies, that he misses 'the best that has been said and thought in the world'—a good deal of that, I must believe, has been subsumed into our modern literatures, one way and another —he will miss, not that, though some of it; but what he will certainly miss is Greek itself, the speech unparalleled, harmonies of prose and verse not to be rendered in any other medium, forms which are themselves meanings. He will miss so a spiritual experience. Scholarship, Greek scholarship, Latin scholarship, any scholarship, fulfils its function to-day as in the past in proportion as it is tutelary of things spiritual.

Printed in the United States
By Bookmasters